MICROSOFT 365

FOR BEGINNERS 2024

MASTERING PRODUCTIVITY TOOLS FOR WORK AND BEYOND

By

Dennis Charles

COPYRIGHT

Printed in the United States of America
© 2024 by Dennis Charles

New Age Publishing
USA | UK | CANADA

TABLE OF CONTENTS

INTRODUCTION

Unlock the full potential of your digital workspace with 'Microsoft 365 For Beginners 2024.' Embark on a journey that promises to transform your approach to productivity, collaboration, and creativity. Within these pages lies the power to streamline your day-to-day tasks, ensuring you're leveraging every tool at your disposal in the most efficient way possible. Imagine the simplicity of mastering your emails, the elegance of crafting compelling presentations, and the satisfaction of managing data with ease. As you flip through the chapters, you'll uncover secrets that elevate your work beyond the mundane, making the complex wonderfully simple.

Let's confront the doubts head-on. You may have tried to use Microsoft 365 before and felt overwhelmed by its complexity. Or maybe you've doubted your ability to keep up with the ever-evolving landscape of digital tools. Here, those fears are addressed by a patient and systematic approach to learning, ensuring that no question goes unanswered and no feature is unexplored.

As you read, allow yourself to envision the transformation that awaits. Picture the newfound confidence as you navigate the Microsoft 365 interface, the ease with which you'll manage tasks that once seemed tedious, and the creativity that will flow as you leverage each application to its fullest. This is not just about learning software; it's about reshaping the way you work, think, and create.

And so, with a commitment to both your success and the power of Microsoft 365, I invite you to dive in. The value you'll gain from this journey is immeasurable, and the life-changing potential of the skills you'll acquire cannot be overstated. Remember, simplicity is the ultimate sophistication, and through this book, sophistication in Microsoft 365 is precisely what you will achieve.

So, are you ready to leave behind the constraints of limited knowledge and step into a realm where proficiency in Microsoft 365 is just a page turn away? The journey toward mastery awaits, and it starts right here, right now. Welcome to 'Microsoft 365 For Beginners'—your passport to a world where your digital workspace becomes a canvas for your creativity and efficiency. Let's begin.

CHAPTER 1 → WELCOME TO "OFFICE" YOUR DIGITAL WORKSPACE

CREATING A MICROSOFT ACCOUNT

Creating an account for Microsoft 365 involves signing up for a Microsoft account and then subscribing to Microsoft 365. Here are the steps to create a Microsoft account and subscribe to Microsoft 365:

Creating a Microsoft Account:

1. **Visit the Microsoft Account Sign-up Page:** Go to the official Microsoft account sign-up page at https://account.microsoft.com.
2. **Click on "Create One":** On the sign-up page, click on the "Create one" link.
3. **Fill in the Required Information:**
    - Enter your email address or create a new one with Outlook.com.
    - Create a strong password.
    - Follow the steps to verify your identity through email or phone.
4. **Complete Profile Information:**
    - Fill in your first and last name.
    - Choose your country/region and date of birth.
    - Click "Next" to continue.

5. **Add Security Information:**
   - Add an alternate email address and/or phone number for security purposes.
   - Optionally, set up two-step verification for added security.
6. **Agree to the Terms:**
   - Read and agree to Microsoft's terms of service and privacy statement.
   - Click "Next."
7. **Welcome to Your New Account:**
   - You'll see a welcome message indicating that your Microsoft account has been created.

Now that you have a Microsoft account, you can proceed to subscribe to Microsoft 365.

Subscribing to Microsoft 365:

1. **Visit the Microsoft 365 Subscription Page:** Go to the official Microsoft 365 subscription page at https://www.microsoft.com/en-us/microsoft-365.
2. **Choose a Plan:**
   - Select the Microsoft 365 plan that best suits your needs (e.g., Microsoft 365 Personal, Microsoft 365 Family, etc.).
   - Click "Buy now" or a similar button.

3. **Sign In:**
    - Sign in with the Microsoft account you created earlier.
4. **Enter Payment Information:**
    - Provide the necessary payment information to complete the subscription process.
5. **Complete the Setup:**
    - Follow any additional prompts to complete the setup process.
    - Download and install the Office apps on your devices.

Congratulations! You've now created a Microsoft account and subscribed to Microsoft 365. You can start using the Office apps and accessing the additional features that come with your subscription.

NAVIGATING THE MICROSOFT 365 INTERFACE

Think of the Microsoft 365 environment as a complex ecosystem, teeming with diverse applications, each serving a specialized function. You will start with a broad overview of the dashboard, the hub of your Microsoft 365 universe, before delving into the intricacies of app navigation and workspace customization.

The Microsoft 365 interface includes various applications and services accessible through web-based interfaces and desktop applications. Here is an overview of some common components of the Microsoft 365 interface:

1. Microsoft 365 Dashboard:

- When you sign in to Microsoft 365, you are typically greeted with a dashboard. This dashboard provides an overview of your info, payment & billings, storage, devices, and other relevant information.

2. App Launcher:

- The App Launcher, also known as the "waffle" icon, is located in the top left corner. Clicking on it opens a menu with icons for various Microsoft 365 applications, such as Outlook, Word, Excel, PowerPoint, OneDrive, and more.

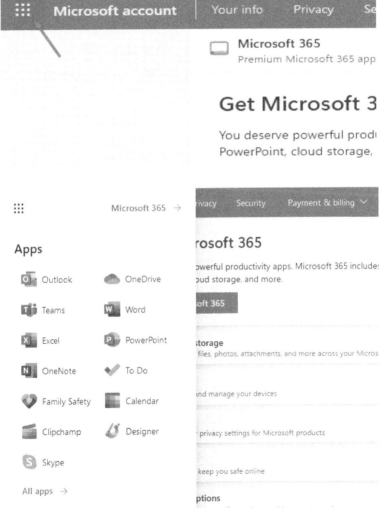

Please note that the interface may evolve, and Microsoft regularly updates its applications and services.

SOME KEY APPLICATIONS WITHIN MICROSOFT 365

Microsoft 365 is a suite of cloud-based productivity tools that include a variety of applications and services designed to enhance collaboration, communication, and productivity within organizations. Here are some of the essential Microsoft 365 apps and their common uses:

1. Outlook:

- **Use:** Email, Calendar, Contacts
- **Features:**
    - Email management and organization
    - Scheduling and managing appointments
    - Contact management

2. Word:

- **Use:** Document creation and editing
- **Features:**
    - Word processing for creating documents
    - Collaboration on documents in real-time
    - Rich formatting and styling options

3. Excel:

- **Use:** Spreadsheet creation and analysis
- **Features:**
  - Data entry and manipulation in cells
  - Formulas and functions for calculations
  - Data visualization through charts and graphs

4. PowerPoint:

- **Use:** Presentation creation and design
- **Features:**
  - Slide creation with text, images, and multimedia
  - Transitions and animations for engaging presentations
  - Collaboration on presentations in real-time

5. OneNote:

- **Use:** Note-taking and collaboration
- **Features:**
  - Digital notebook for capturing and organizing notes
  - Support for text, images, audio, and sketches
  - Collaboration on shared notebooks

6. Teams:

- **Use:** Collaboration and communication

- **Features:**
  - Chat for instant messaging
  - Video and audio meetings
  - Collaboration on files and documents
  - Integration with other Microsoft 365 apps

7. OneDrive:

- **Use:** Cloud storage and file sharing
- **Features:**
  - Personal and shared file storage in the cloud
  - Version history and file recovery
  - Real-time collaboration on Office documents

8. SharePoint:

- **Use:** Document management and collaboration
- **Features:**
  - Team sites for collaboration
  - Document libraries for version-controlled file storage
  - Integration with other Microsoft 365 apps

9. Planner:

- **Use:** Task and project management
- **Features:**
  - Task creation and assignment
  - Visual boards for tracking progress

- Collaboration on project plans

10. Yammer:

- **Use:** Enterprise social networking
- **Features:**
    - Social platform for communication and collaboration
    - Group discussions and announcements
    - Integration with other Microsoft 365 apps

11. Forms:

- **Use:** Survey and form creation
- **Features:**
    - Create surveys, quizzes, and forms
    - Collect responses and analyze results
    - Integration with other Microsoft 365 apps

12. Power Automate:

- **Use:** Workflow automation
- **Features:**
    - Automate repetitive tasks and processes
    - Create workflows that connect different apps and services

13. Power BI:

- **Use:** Business intelligence and analytics

- **Features:**
  - Create interactive dashboards and reports
  - Visualize and analyze data from various sources

These are just some of the key applications within Microsoft 365. The suite is designed to provide a comprehensive set of tools for businesses and individuals to enhance productivity, communication, and collaboration in a cloud-based environment.

CHAPTER 2 → WORD IN THE CLOUD: CRAFTING DOCUMENTS

STARTING FROM SCRATCH: CREATING A NEW DOCUMENT

Embarking on the journey of crafting a new document in Microsoft 365's Word can be as exhilarating as the first stroke of a painter's brush across a blank canvas. The promise of a crisp, unmarked page awaits your ideas, ready to be transformed into text, tables, and images that convey your message with clarity and style.

Let us delve into the initial movement. Open Word from the Microsoft 365 suite. To do this, click on the "App Launcher" icon at the top left of the Microsoft 365 interface and choose Word.

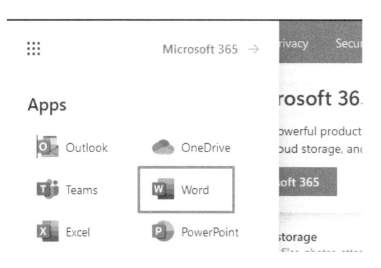

After choosing "Word", you are presented with various options. You can choose to open a blank document, template or recently opened document. Blank document opens a fresh document canvas devoid of any pre-existing content or formatting, templates allow you to start with professionally designed layouts and recently opened documents provide quick access to files that have been recently accessed or modified.

If it's your first encounter, take a moment to admire the sleek design, the ribbon of tools awaiting your command, and the subtle invitation of the blank document icon.

Now, let's wade deeper, shall we? Upon initiating Word, you are greeted by the Start screen—think of it as your gateway to creation. From here, you can opt for a blank document or foray into the world of templates. But let's not get ahead of ourselves. Select 'Blank Document' and feel the anticipation build as the new document springs forth.

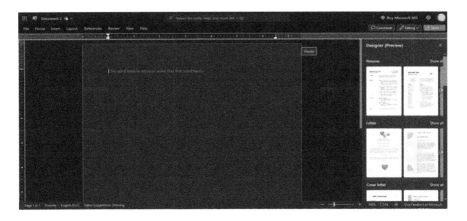

As you stand at the threshold of creation, a myriad of tools and features lay before you. The ribbon stretches across the top, a tapestry of possibilities with tabs like 'Home', 'Insert', and 'Design'. Each tab is a chest of tools, and each tool is a key to unlocking different elements of your document.

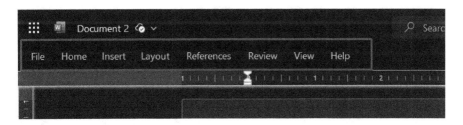

Beware, though—overzealous clicking can lead to a cluttered mess. Approach the ribbon with the precision of a jeweller, selecting only what you need when you need it.

As you continue, you might ponder, "How do I know if I'm on the right track?" Simple. Your document takes shape with each sentence crafted, each image inserted, and each table aligned. The canvas responds to your touch, the text wrapping elegantly around inserted graphics, the headings standing proud.

Should you encounter a misstep—a misplaced image, a stubborn bullet list—fret not. The 'Undo' button is your silent guardian, always one click away from erasing the last action, giving you the freedom to experiment without fear. Alternatively, you can use the keyboard shortcut 'Ctrl + Z' to undo an action.

You may also wonder, "What if the interface seems overwhelming?" Remember, the 'Search box' feature at the top of the interface is your guiding star. Type what you wish to do in the box with the light bulb icon, and let it illuminate your path with suggestions and commands.

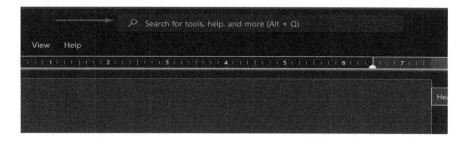

Templates, those pre-designed wonders, await your command in Word's repository. They offer a shortcut to professional layouts for resumes, newsletters, and more. A template can be a beacon, guiding you through the fog of design choices.

But tread lightly here, for not all templates are created equal. Some may dazzle with their design but falter in functionality. Choose one that resonates with your project's spirit and allows you to tailor it to your narrative.

On your right are different templates for your use. If you do not see any, click the 'Home' tab and click 'Designer' to show various templates you can work with.

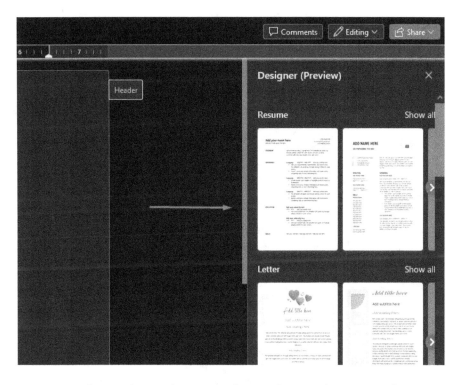

Once you've selected a template, the real artistry begins. Replace the placeholder text with your own eloquent words. Swap out stock images for visuals that speak your truth. Adjust color schemes to reflect the tone of your message.

Now, pause and reflect. Does the rhythm of your text ebb and flow with ease? Is the visual harmony of your layout pleasing to the eye? If you hesitated, even for a heartbeat, revisit your choices. Adjust, refine, and perfect.

In the end, when you print or share your document, the satisfaction of a job well done will be palpable. It's not just a file you've created; it's a piece of your intellect, preserved in digital form, ready to be shared with the world.

Proceed to give the document a name by clicking on the default name, which could be 'Document 1' or 'Document 2' and so on. Then, you can rename the document and choose a location to save.

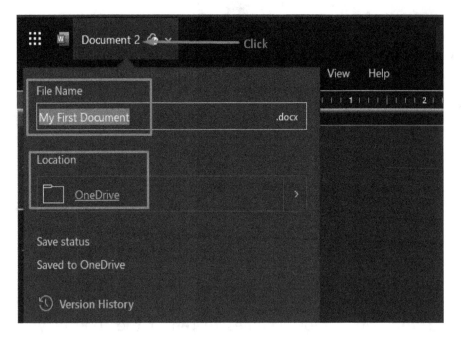

And so, with these steps, you transform a blank screen into a document that breathes purpose. You've not only started from scratch but created something with permanence and presence. You, my friend, have mastered the art of creating a new document in Microsoft 365's Word.

FORMAT WITH FLAIR: STYLING YOUR DOCUMENT

In the alchemy of document creation, mere words are the base metals, while styling and design elements are the elusive philosopher's stone, capable of transforming the mundane into the magnificent. Your quest, noble scribe, is to harness the arcane secrets of Microsoft 365's Word to make your document not just informative but also visually arresting.

You'll need your Word processor, a dash of creativity, and an eye for design. The prerequisite is a basic understanding of Word, as elaborated upon in the previous chapter, and a document that cries out for transformation from a caterpillar of content into a butterfly of brilliance.

Picture a map spread before you, each landmark a step in your journey of styling. This journey includes choosing text styles, inserting and formatting images, and adorning your document with captivating design elements.

Let us embark on this trek with the first stride: the art of text styling. Delve into the 'Home' tab's trove and behold the array of fonts, each with a personality as distinct as the stars in the night sky. From the professional poise of Arial to the whim of Comic Sans, choose a font that speaks the language of your document's soul.

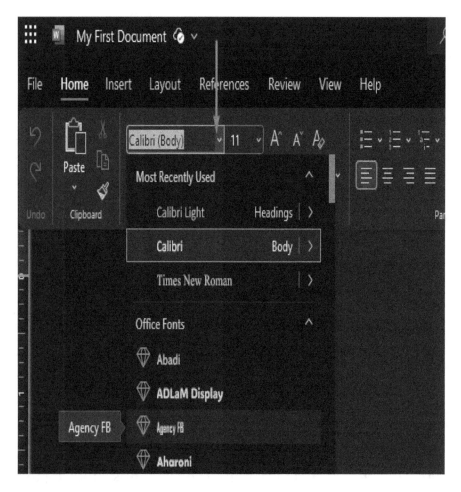

Next, set your headings apart with the magic of styles. A heading is not merely text; it's a herald announcing the forthcoming content. Apply 'Heading 1' for main titles, 'Heading 2' for subheadings, and so on, creating a hierarchy that guides the reader through your narrative labyrinth.

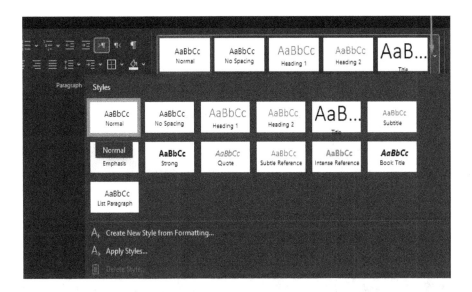

Are you wondering how to make your text not just speak but sing? Vary the font size to create a chorus of visual cues, leading your audience from one verse of your document to the next. Bold and italics are your crescendos and decrescendos, emphasizing key notes in the melody of your message.

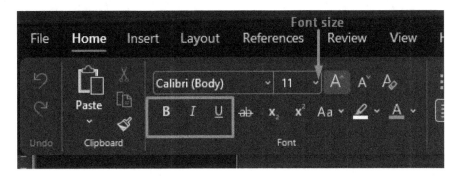

But beware, the path is fraught with potential pitfalls. A document clad in too many fonts is like a crowd speaking in tongues—chaos. Restraint, dear author, is your watchword. Choose two, perhaps three fonts at most, and let them dance together in harmonious typography.

Now, let's turn our gaze to the realm of imagery. Click 'Insert', then 'Pictures', and summon visuals that echo your theme. Wrap text around images with the grace of a practiced poet, ensuring each paragraph flows seamlessly around the art.

Yet even here, dragons lurk. An image too large overwhelms the text, while one too small becomes lost. Resize with care, hold down 'Shift' to maintain proportions, and always respect the balance between word and picture.

And what of design elements, you ask? Borders, shading, and colors await your command. They are the spices in your document's dish, to be sprinkled with a judicious hand. A border frames your page, shading highlights a poignant passage, and a splash of color can wake a weary reader.

To validate your efforts, step back and view your creation through the eyes of a stranger. Is it a feast for the eyes? Does it guide the reader with invisible threads from beginning to end? If doubts cloud your vision, tweak and tune until your document sings a clear tune.

In the shadowed corners where troubles brew, you might find images rebelling against their text-wrapped chains or styles that refuse to behave. Fear not. Right-click the rogue element, summon the 'Format' dialog, and negotiate terms of compliance. Remember, 'Undo' is your ally, ever ready to revert an errant action.

Let us conclude with a flourish. Your document, once a drab collection of words, now stands proud, arrayed in the finery of fonts, the jewels of imagery, and the embroidery of design elements. It's not merely a document; it's a tapestry woven from the threads of your creativity, ready to captivate all who gaze upon it.

With this tome of knowledge, you are equipped to set forth and adorn your documents with the flair they deserve. Go forth, for you are not a mere user of Word—you are an artisan, and your documents are the canvas upon which you shall paint masterpieces.

COLLABORATE AND SHARE: WORKING WITH OTHERS

In an era where the boundaries of office walls have been stretched across continents, collaboration emerges as the golden thread that weaves disparate efforts into a singular tapestry of success. It's in the heart of this digital renaissance that Microsoft 365 presents itself not just as a suite of tools but as a conduit for collective synergy.

The modern workplace is no stranger to the challenges of teamwork, especially when it comes to document management. Picture a team scattered across time zones, each member with their own set of skills, all aiming to contribute to a single document. Herein lies the crux of the problem: How do we marry individual contributions into a coherent whole without succumbing to the chaos of conflicting versions and the cacophony of endless email attachments?

Left unchecked, this problem can spiral into a vortex of inefficiency, with precious hours lost to sorting out which version is the latest or who has the right to edit what.

Imagine the frustration of working on a document for hours, only to discover that your colleague has done the same, rendering one of your efforts obsolete. The consequences of such disarray range from missed deadlines to the erosion of team morale.

But fear not, for within Microsoft 365 lies the solution—co-authoring in real-time. Imagine a world where your document lives in the cloud, accessible and editable by all team members simultaneously. Changes appear as they are made, with each author's input neatly sectioned off by color-coded cursors dancing across the screen. This is not a distant dream; it is the reality offered by Microsoft 365's powerful collaboration features.

To harness this collaborative magic, begin by saving your document to OneDrive or SharePoint. Invite your colleagues to join the fray by sharing the document directly from within the application—Word, Excel, or PowerPoint. Set permissions with a few clicks, deciding who can edit and who can view. The implementation is as straightforward as it is elegant.

Here's a step-by-step guide on how to collaborate and share documents using Word 365:

Real-Time Collaboration:

1. Open a Document:

- Open the Word document you want to collaborate on in Word 365.

2. Share the Document:
   - Click on the "Share" button in the upper right corner of the Word interface.

3. Invite Collaborators:
   - Enter the email addresses of the people you want to collaborate with. You can also copy a link and share it manually.

4. Set Permissions:
   - Choose the permission level for each collaborator. Options include "Can edit" or "Can view."

5. Send Invitations:
   - Click "Send" to send invitations to your collaborators. They will receive an email notification with a link to the document.

6. Collaborate in Real-Time:
   - Once your collaborators open the document, you can all work on it simultaneously. Edits made by one person are instantly reflected in others.

Document Sharing and Link Generation:

1. Open a Document:
   - Open the Word document you want to share in Word 365.

2. Click on "File":
    - Click on the "File" tab in the top left corner of the Word interface.
3. Select "Share":
    - Choose the "Share" option from the menu.
4. Generate a Sharing Link:
    - Click on "Copy Link" to generate a shareable link to the document. You can choose the access level for the link (e.g., "Anyone with the link can edit" or "Anyone with the link can view").
5. Send the Link:
    - Share the link via email, chat, or any other communication method with the people you want to share the document with.
6. Control Access:
    - If you want to control access, you can also use the "People in your organization" option to share with specific people within your organization.

Comments and Annotations:

1. Highlight Text:
    - Select a portion of text you want to comment on or annotate.
2. Insert a Comment:

- o Right-click on the selected text and choose "New Comment." Alternatively, go to the "Review" tab and click on "New Comment."
3. Collaborate through Comments:
   - o Collaborators can reply to comments, and discussions can happen directly within the document.

Version History:

1. Access Version History:
   - o Click on the "File" tab, select "Info," and click on "Version History."
2. Review Changes:
   - o You can review changes made by collaborators, revert to a previous version, and see who made specific modifications.

By following these steps, you can effectively collaborate and share documents in Word 365, making it easier to work together with colleagues or team members in real time.

CHAPTER 3 → EXCEL: THE NUMBER CRUNCHER'S DELIGHT

EXCEL BASICS: CREATING YOUR FIRST SPREADSHEET

Embarking on the journey of mastering Microsoft Excel can feel akin to setting sail across a vast digital ocean. With its myriad of functions and capabilities, Excel within Microsoft 365 is a powerful tool essential for managing data in today's world. Your quest begins with a single step: creating your first spreadsheet. By following a sequence of straightforward steps, you'll achieve the gratifying objective of transforming a blank canvas into a structured array of information.

Before diving into the world of cells and formulas, ensure you have a stable Internet. You can then click on the App launcher and choose Excel to launch it. Along the way, you'll discover the functions that make Excel indispensable for data organization and analysis.

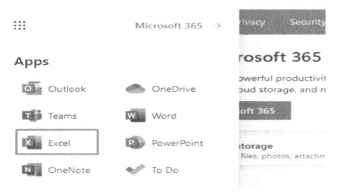

Firstly, open Excel from your Microsoft 365 suite. You'll be greeted by a splash screen presenting various templates. For our purpose, select 'Blank Workbook' to start fresh. Now, gaze upon the grid of cells; this is where your data will reside. Each cell is a receptacle for information, defined by a column letter and a row number.

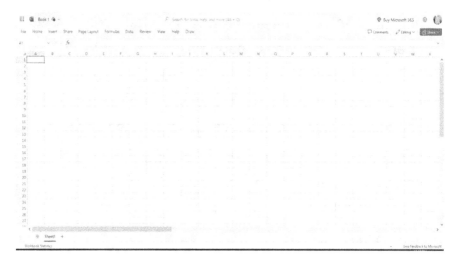

Let's begin populating this grid. Click on a cell, any cell, and type in your first piece of data. Press 'Enter' or 'Tab' to move to the next cell and continue inputting information. As you fill in the cells, notice how Excel anticipates your movement, guiding you along the rows and columns.

Here's a handy tip: if you're entering data that follows a pattern, such as dates or sequences, input the first few items, highlight them, and then drag the fill handle (a small square at the cell's bottom-right corner) downwards or across. Excel will magically extend the sequence for you.

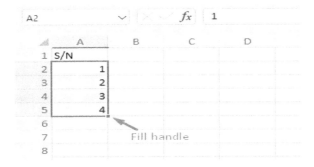

But beware! Accidentally overwriting data is a common pitfall. Always double-check the cell you're about to edit, especially if it contains formulas or critical information.

As you populate your spreadsheet, you can adjust the column width or row height for better readability. Hover over the line separating the column headers or row numbers, click and drag to your desired dimension.

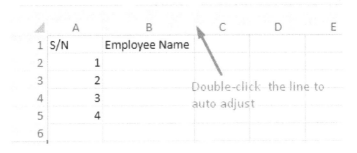

Excel also allows you to format text with bold, italics, or different colors, adding clarity and emphasis to important data. All these can be achieved in the 'Home' tab.

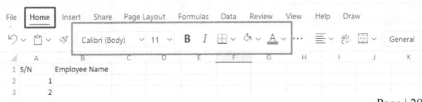

But how do you know if you've done it right? Validation comes through the visual harmony of your data and the ease of navigation across the spreadsheet. Test this by scrolling through your data, ensuring that everything is visible and well-organized. You should also experiment with basic formulas, such as SUM, to ensure they return the expected results.

Suppose you encounter a roadblock like a formula not working as expected. Don't despair! Troubleshooting is part of the learning process. A common issue is incorrect cell references in formulas. Double-check your formula syntax and the cells it references. Excel's formula auditing tools can be invaluable in these situations, helping to trace and correct errors.

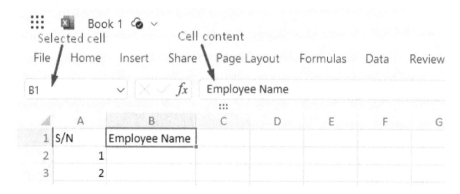

Remember, practice makes perfect. With each new spreadsheet, your confidence and proficiency will grow. Embrace the journey, remain curious, and your spreadsheets will soon become a canvas for creativity and efficiency.

In conclusion, allow yourself to marvel at the symphony of cells before you, each one humming with potential. With the foundation laid in this chapter, you're well on your way to harnessing the power of Excel within the Microsoft 365 suite. Always remember that the most complex spreadsheets begin with a single cell. What will you create with yours?

FORMULAS AND FUNCTIONS: THE MAGIC BEHIND THE CELLS

Welcome to the next chapter in your exploration of Microsoft Excel within Microsoft 365. As you've become familiar with the initial steps of creating and formatting a spreadsheet, it's time to delve into the heart of Excel's power—its ability to perform calculations and analyze data with ease and precision.

Imagine standing before a vast library, each book brimming with knowledge. In Excel, formulas and functions are like these books, each containing specific instructions to process your data. They are the tools that transform static numbers into dynamic information, providing insights and answers to complex questions with the click of a button.

At the core of Excel's utility belt are formulas, which are expressions that perform calculations on your data. They are crafted using operators such as addition (+), subtraction (-), multiplication (*), and division (/). Formulas can be as simple as '=A1+A2' or as complex as you need them to be, combining multiple operations and cells.

Let's consider a practical example to illustrate this. Suppose you're tracking expenses for a project. By entering '=SUM(C2:C5)', Excel sums the total expenses listed from cell C2 to C5. This simple formula is a fundamental skill in Excel, allowing you to add up a range of numbers quickly.

C6			✓	✕ ✓	fx	=SUM(C2:C5)	

	A	B	C	D
1	S/N	Product purchased	Expenses	
2	1	Iron bar	200	
3	2	Cement	150	
4	3	Wood	200	
5	4	Gravel	300	
6			=SUM(C2:C5)	
7				

But what if you need more than just a sum? Functions come into play here. Functions are predefined formulas that perform specific calculations using particular values, known as arguments, in a specific order. Excel boasts a wide array of functions, each categorized by its purpose – from financial calculations to text manipulation and beyond.

Dive deeper, and you'll discover functions like 'AVERAGE' to find the mean value, 'MAX' to identify the highest number in a range, and 'VLOOKUP' to search for a piece of data in a table. Each function requires you to understand its particular syntax and arguments. For instance, 'AVERAGE(C2:C5)' calculates the mean of the values in cells B2 through B5.

It's important to remember that functions can be combined and nested within each other to solve more intricate problems. Can you picture a chef expertly combining ingredients to create a gourmet dish? Similarly, you can mix and match functions and formulas to cook up the perfect solution to your data challenges.

Consider the following scenario: You have a list of sales figures, and you want to calculate the average sales, but only for those that are above a certain threshold. Here, you might use a combination of the 'AVERAGE' and 'IF' functions to create a formula that selectively averages the data.

To enhance the richness of the text, let's integrate a quote from an Excel enthusiast: "Mastering Excel's formulas and functions is like learning a new language—a language of numbers that, once fluent, allows you to converse with your data in profound ways."

When you encounter terms like 'relative' and 'absolute' cell references, do not be daunted. These terms are vital when you want to copy formulas across cells. A relative reference, like 'A1', changes when copied to another cell, maintaining the relationship to the original cell. An absolute reference, such as 'A1', remains constant, no matter where it's copied. This distinction is crucial for accurate calculations.

As you progress, you will likely stumble upon functions that may seem enigmatic, like 'INDEX' and 'MATCH'. But as with any complex subject, breaking it down into simpler components makes it manageable. 'INDEX' returns the value of a cell within a table based on the row and column numbers you specify. 'MATCH', on the other hand, finds the position of a specified item in a range.

To conclude, the journey through Excel's formulas and functions is a transformative one. Each formula you learn and each function you master adds to your analytical prowess, turning data into actionable insights. Remember, Excel is not just about handling data—it's about unlocking the stories the data tells.

So, what's the key takeaway from this chapter? The magic of Excel lies in its ability to perform complex tasks through formulas and functions, making it an indispensable tool for anyone looking to make data-driven decisions. Embrace the challenge, and you'll soon see the magic unfold in your very own cells.

CHARTS AND GRAPHS: VISUALIZING DATA

Visualizing data is akin to translating a foreign language into a universal tongue, one that can be understood at a glance by anyone, irrespective of their expertise in data analysis. The goal here is to guide you through the art and science of creating charts and graphs in Microsoft 365, specifically in Excel, transforming raw data into visual insights that tell a compelling story.

To embark on this journey, you'll need a basic understanding of Excel, including basic formatting skills and how to enter data into a spreadsheet. Additionally, ensure you have a dataset ready for visualization and access to the Excel application, part of the Microsoft 365 suite.

Before diving into the nitty-gritty, picture a map. A map is a visual representation of data—geographical data, to be exact. Similarly, charts and graphs serve as maps guiding viewers through numerical data landscapes. They can reveal trends, highlight relationships, and communicate complex data in a straightforward, visually appealing manner.

Now, let us break down the process into detailed steps:

1. Selecting the Right Type of Chart:

- Begin by understanding your data and the story you want it to tell. Is it a comparison, a distribution, a composition, or a relationship you wish to showcase?

- Choose a chart type that best represents your data's narrative—bar charts for comparisons, line graphs for trends over time, pie charts for showing parts of a whole, and scatter plots for observing relationships.

2. Preparing Your Data:

- Organize your data clearly and concisely. Data should be sorted and, if necessary, calculated before you attempt to create a chart.

- Ensure that your dataset is complete and error-free. Missing or incorrect data can lead to misleading charts.

3. Creating a Chart:

- Highlight the data range you want to include in the chart.

	A	B	C	D	E	F
1	S/N	Product purchased	Expenses			
2		1 Iron bar	200			
3		2 Cement	150			
4		3 Wood	200			
5		4 Gravel	300			
6		5 Paint	600			
7		6 Electric Wire	500			
8		7 Fire Alarm	400			
9						

- Navigate to the 'Insert' tab and select the type of chart you wish to create.

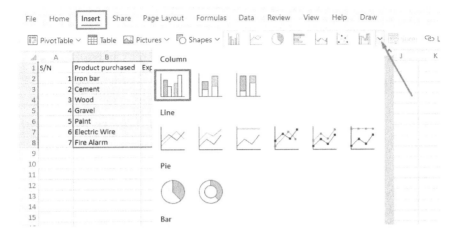

- Excel will automatically generate a chart based on your selected data.

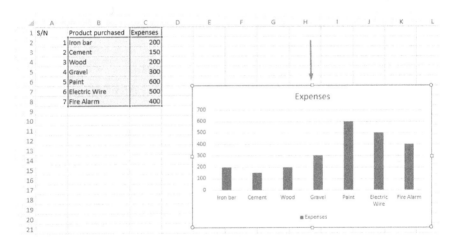

4. Customizing Your Chart:

- Adjust the chart title, axis labels, and legend for clarity and impact by clicking any of the components in the chart.

- Use color and style to enhance readability, but avoid overcomplicating the visual with too many effects.

5. Interpreting Your Chart:

- Take a moment to review the visual. Does it tell the story you intended?

- Look for trends, patterns, and outliers. These insights are the value extracted from your raw data.

Throughout the process, consider these tips and warnings:

- Simplicity is key. A cluttered chart can be as confusing as a table full of numbers.

- Ensure that your chart's scale and axes are appropriate for the data being presented. Misleading scales can distort the data's story.

- Be mindful of the colors you choose; colorblindness can affect how some users perceive your charts.

To validate your work, ask yourself or a colleague if the chart conveys the intended message clearly and accurately. If what the data is showing is not immediately obvious, you may need to make some adjustments.

If you encounter issues, such as data not displaying correctly or the chart type not representing the data as you expected, troubleshoot by checking your data range and ensuring that the chart type is suitable for your data. Sometimes, switching to a different chart type or adjusting the data selection can resolve these problems.

Your journey through data visualization in Excel does not end here; it's a continuous path of discovery and learning. With each chart you create, you hone your skills, becoming a more effective storyteller. Remember, the power of a well-crafted chart is immense—it can turn data into insight and insight into action.

In conclusion, the essence of data visualization is to illuminate the unseen to make the complex accessible. As you progress, keep experimenting with different types of charts and graphs, and watch as your data begins to speak with clarity and purpose. Excel is not just a tool for calculations—it's a canvas for your data stories.

CHAPTER 4 → POWERPOINT: PRESENTATIONS THAT PERSUADE

BUILDING YOUR FIRST PRESENTATION

Stepping onto the stage of digital storytelling, your first PowerPoint presentation awaits its creation. Imagine captivating an audience with a seamless blend of words and images, all at the click of a button. That's the goal - to craft a presentation that not only informs but also engages and impresses.

Before embarking on this creative journey, you'll need a few things in hand. Ensure you have Microsoft 365 installed on your computer, a clear idea of your presentation topic, and any content or images you wish to include. With these at the ready, you're set to begin.

Envision the process of crafting a tapestry, where each thread is a slide contributing to the grand design. We'll start with the canvas - the PowerPoint interface - and gradually add the colors and patterns - your slides, text, and designs.

Diving into the details, let's ignite the engine of PowerPoint. Open PowerPoint from the Microsoft 365 suite. To do this, click on the "App Launcher" icon at the top left of the Microsoft 365 interface and choose PowerPoint.

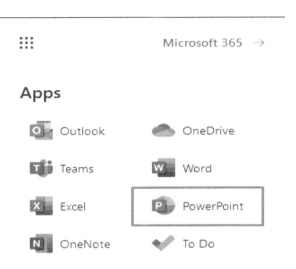

Upon opening the application, you're greeted by a selection of templates. Each one offers a unique aesthetic that can set the tone for your presentation. Do you go with the bold and modern or the subtle and professional? Take a moment. Let your content guide the choice, for the design should echo the voice of your message.

With a template chosen, the foundation is laid. Now, the slides beckon to be built. The first slide is your introduction – your handshake to the audience. Here, you state the presentation's purpose and perhaps tease what's to come. Remember, first impressions linger, so make it count.

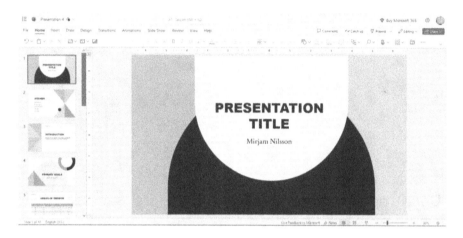

Use other slides in the templates to build up your presentation. As you proceed, you might need to add more slides. Adding slides is as simple as a click on the 'New Slide' button.

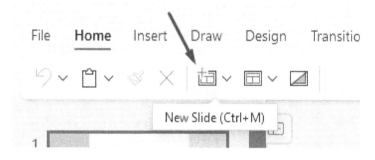

Now, choose a layout for the new slide by clicking 'Slide Layout' in the Home ribbon.

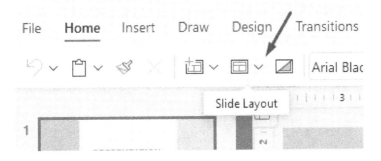

Each new slide is a blank canvas awaiting your ideas. Will this slide present a bullet list of key points or perhaps a striking image with a quote? Vary the slide content to keep your audience engaged; a monotone presentation risks losing their attention.

As you populate slides with content, consider the layout. Balance text and visuals to create a harmonious flow. Too much text can overwhelm you, while too many images may dilute your message.

Here's a tip: less is often more. Use bullet points to distil information to its essence. Choose images that complement the text, not compete with it. And remember to make use of PowerPoint's alignment tools to keep your slides tidy and professional-looking.

But what if the text seems dull or the images lackluster? Worry not. PowerPoint offers a range of formatting options. Highlight key phrases by bolding or changing the font color. Enhance images with borders or effects. These subtle embellishments can make your content pop. The

Home ribbon contains the necessary tools for formatting text in PowerPoint.

What of warnings? Beware the siren call of flashy transitions and animations. Used sparingly, they can emphasize a point or signal a shift in topic. Overused, they become distractions, upstaging your content.

How will you know if your presentation hits the mark? Practice and preview. Run through the slides, refining them as you go. Is each slide clear and purposeful? Does the overall story flow? This rehearsal is your litmus test.

If you encounter hiccups, such as inconsistent formatting or a slide that refuses to cooperate, don't despair. The troubleshooting gods smile upon the persistent. Seek out the 'Help' feature in PowerPoint or look online for solutions. Many have navigated these waters before you and left behind a trail of tips and fixes.

In the end, your presentation stands as a testament to your message. It should be a cohesive blend of clarity and creativity, ready to inform and inspire.

Have you captured the essence of your topic? Have you transported your audience on a visual journey they'll remember? If you can answer 'yes', you've not only built a presentation; you've created an experience.

And so, as the final slide fades and the applause begins, you'll know the effort was worthwhile. This is but the first of many stories you'll tell through the lens of PowerPoint, each one an opportunity to refine your craft and enchant your audience anew.

ADDING MULTIMEDIA: IMAGES, VIDEOS, AND AUDIO

In the realm of presentations, the inclusion of multimedia elements like images, videos, and audio can transform a simple slide show into an immersive experience, capturing the essence of your message and leaving a lasting impression on your audience. That's the beacon we're heading towards – a multimedia-rich presentation that resonates with every viewer.

To embark on this adventure, you will need a few essentials: a stable internet connection for accessing online multimedia resources and any existing images, audio files, or videos you wish to incorporate. Ensure that all multimedia files are compatible with PowerPoint and legally permissible for use.

Imagine yourself as a director of a film where each scene is meticulously crafted. We begin with a single frame – the

PowerPoint slide – and slowly weave in the layers of visual and auditory stimuli that will captivate your audience.

Let's unfold the narrative of adding multimedia step by step. A broad overview paints a scene where you first insert an image, then a video clip, followed by an audio track, adjusting each to fit perfectly within the tapestry of your presentation.

To start, select the slide you wish to adorn with an image. Click on the 'Insert' tab, choose 'Pictures,' and browse to find the image that encapsulates your message. Once placed, you can drag the corners to resize or use the formatting options to add artistic effects, borders, or shadows.

As you weave in visual elements, consider the narrative rhythm. Does the image echo the tempo of your words? Or does it shout over the subtleties of your message?

Placement and formatting are key. Position your image so it complements, not competes with text. An image behind text should be faded to ensure readability.

Now, imagine the impact of a video. To insert one, navigate to the 'Insert' tab again, but this time select 'Video.' You can choose a file from your computer or an online video. Once inserted, right-click on the video to trim its length, add a fade in or fade out, and ensure it's set to play when you desire, be it automatically or when clicked.

A word of caution, though. Videos can be double-edged swords – they must be wielded with precision. Ensure that the video's content is directly relevant to your slide, and keep it short to maintain your audience's attention.

What about audio? The whisper of background music or the clarity of a voice-over can stir emotions and underscore your message. Add audio by selecting 'Audio' from the 'Insert' tab, choosing your file, and setting it to play across slides or only when triggered.

Here's a tip: balance is vital. Just like the ebb and flow of a melody, the interplay between text, images, and sound should be harmonious. More loudly and softly, and the audience may miss the essence of your message.

How do you know if the multimedia elements are enhancing your presentation or overwhelming it? Test it. Play the slides as if you are in the audience, and you can do this by clicking the 'Present' Button at the top right of the interface. Do the transitions from text to image to video feel seamless? Is the audio clear and at the right volume? This testing phase is crucial for polishing your presentation to perfection.

Should you encounter any glitches, such as a video not playing or audio that's out of sync, do not let frustration cloud your vision. Troubleshooting is part of the journey. PowerPoint's help feature is a treasure trove of solutions, and online forums are bustling with fellow creators who have faced and overcome similar challenges.

In the end, your multimedia-enriched presentation should flow like a river – natural, engaging, and leading the audience through the landscape of your narrative. It's more than a collection of slides; it's an artful blend of sights and sounds that, together, tell a compelling story.

Have the images painted the picture you intended? Do the videos bring motion to your message? Does the audio amplify the emotion? If the answer is 'yes,' then you've mastered the art of multimedia in presentations.

As the screen dims and the final notes of your audio fade out, the silence in the room is not empty – it's full of the impact your presentation has made. You've not just informed; you've transported your audience to a place where your message lives and breathes. And that, dear creator, is the true power of multimedia in storytelling.

ANIMATING YOUR SLIDES: TRANSITIONS AND EFFECTS

Have you ever watched a presentation where each slide seems to come alive, captivating your attention from start to finish? That's the magic of well-executed transitions and animations in PowerPoint. By the end of this chapter, you will have mastered the art of adding dynamism to your presentations, ensuring your audience remains not just attentive but thoroughly engaged.

Before we dive in, let's ensure you have everything you need. A presentation in progress and a creative mindset are your primary tools. Familiarity with PowerPoint's basic functions is helpful but not essential—we'll cover everything step by step.

Imagine your slides as actors on a stage, transitioning from one scene to the next with grace and purpose. This is our goal: to choreograph the movement between slides and the elements within them so that they support and enhance your narrative.

The roadmap ahead is clear. We start with a broad overview, introducing the concept of transitions—how one slide gives way to the next. Then, we'll explore animations, the individual movements within a slide. After that, we jump into the detailed steps to apply these effects, followed by practical tips and warnings to bear in mind. Finally, we'll discuss how to test your animations and transitions to ensure they work flawlessly.

Let's delve deeper now. Transitions are the effects that occur when moving from one slide to another. They can be as simple as a fade or as intricate as a three-dimensional flip. To apply a transition, click on the 'Transitions' tab in PowerPoint and choose from the gallery. Click on 'Present' to see how it looks before applying it to your slides.

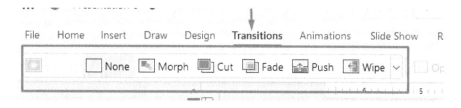

Animations, on the other hand, are about the elements within a slide. They can enter with a bounce, emphasize with a spin, or exit with a swoosh. To animate an object, select it and go to the 'Animations' tab. Here, you can pick from various effects—entrance, emphasis, or exit. Again, use 'Present' to see the animation in action.

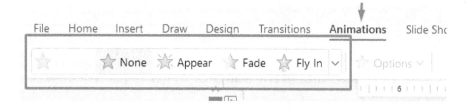

Do you sense the choreography taking shape? Now, let's precisely orchestrate each movement. Select the object you wish to animate and click on 'Add Animation.' You can stack multiple animations on a single object for a compound effect. Use the 'Animation Pane' to adjust timing and order, ensuring a smooth performance.

Remember that transitions and animations are the spices of your presentation—used wisely, they enhance; used excessively, they overpower. Here are some tips: keep transitions consistent and use animations to highlight key points. Be cautious not to overdo it; the focus should remain on your message, not the special effects.

But how do you know if your efforts hit the mark? Test your slides. Watch the entire presentation to feel the rhythm and flow. Are the transitions smooth? Do the animations serve the narrative? This validation step is crucial for a polished final product.

Should you run into trouble—perhaps an animation doesn't start as planned, or a transition seems jarring— don't despair. Troubleshooting is often as simple as revisiting the 'Animation Pane' to adjust timings or consulting PowerPoint's 'Help' function to clarify functions you may not fully understand.

As you wrap up, ask yourself: Do the animations and transitions contribute to the story I'm telling? They should feel like natural extensions of your message, guiding your audience through your presentation with clarity and impact.

In conclusion, mastering transitions and animations in PowerPoint is akin to learning a new language—the language of visual storytelling. When done right, your slides will not just convey information; they will resonate with the audience, leaving a memorable impression long after the presentation concludes. And that, dear presenter, is the true art of bringing your slides to life.

CHAPTER 5 → OUTLOOK: COMMUNICATION CENTRAL

MASTERING EMAIL: SENDING AND RECEIVING

In the digital age, the art of communication hinges greatly on mastering the tools at our disposal. Among these, email stands as a modern-day marvel, a bridge connecting us across vast digital landscapes. As you embark on this journey through 'Microsoft 365 For Beginners', you shall conquer the realm of electronic mail, transforming your inbox from a daunting maze into a bastion of efficiency.

Your quest is clear—to become adept at composing, sending, receiving, and organizing emails. By the end of this chapter, the once murky waters of email etiquette and management will seem like a tranquil pond, inviting and serene.

Before we set sail, ensure you have an active Microsoft 365 account, a stable internet connection, a keen mind for detail, and a willingness to learn. Open Outlook from the Microsoft 365 suite. To do this, click on the "App Launcher" icon at the top left of the Microsoft 365 interface and choose Outlook.

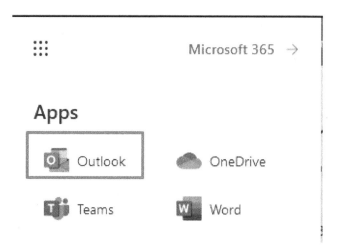

Sending mails

First, let us explore the composition of an email. The 'New Mail' button is your beacon—click it to reveal a blank canvas awaiting your input.

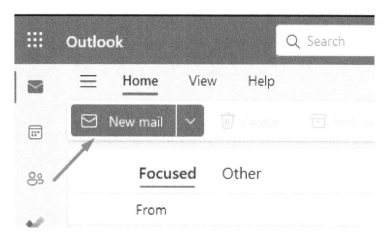

Start by addressing your email to a specific recipient; type their email address into the 'To' field with precision, for a misplaced letter could send your message adrift into the void.

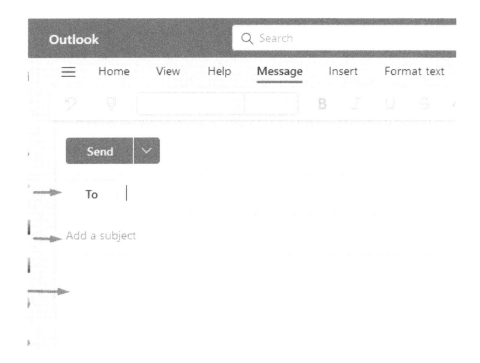

The 'Subject' line is the flag atop your mast, signaling the purpose of your message. Keep it concise yet informative; a well-crafted subject line is a herald of the content within.

Now, the body of your message is where your thoughts take form. Begin with a courteous greeting, setting the tone for a respectful exchange. As your fingers dance across the keyboard, remember that clarity is king. Each sentence should be a stepping stone, guiding the reader through your message. Use paragraphs to group related thoughts, just as the stars form constellations in the night sky.

Attached is the cargo of your vessel carrying additional information. To attach a file, seek the paperclip icon, a symbol of binding documents to your message. Choose your files wisely, ensuring they are neither too heavy to load nor too numerous to overwhelm.

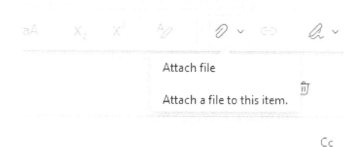

A word of caution—beware the sirens of haste. Proofread your email before releasing it into the digital winds. Typos and grammatical errors are like hidden reefs that can sink the credibility of your message.

Send a test email to yourself. This act of self-reflection ensures your message appears as intended. The formatting should be pristine, the attachments accessible, and the content should be free from the tangles of confusion.

Should trouble arise—a recipient not found, an attachment too large—do not despair. Most issues cast a shadow in the form of error messages. Heed their warnings, adjust your course, and try again.

Receiving mails

As you delve into receiving emails, the glow of a new message will signal an arrival. Open it with a click and peruse its contents with a discerning eye. Your inbox is your harbor; keep it orderly with folders and categories, just as a captain maintains a tidy ship.

To master your email is to master a key skill in the tapestry of modern communication. With each message sent and received, you weave your thread into the digital fabric, connecting with others in a dance of pixels and text. Embrace this power, for it will serve you well in the boundless realms of Microsoft 365.

Remember, an efficient inbox is not a destination but a journey—one of continuous learning and adaptation. As you close this chapter, you stand at the helm, a seasoned navigator of the email seas, ready to chart your course in the vast ocean of digital communication.

CALENDAR MANAGEMENT: SCHEDULING MADE SIMPLE

Imagine a world where every plan, every meeting, and every reminder aligns in harmonious synchronicity. Envision a life where time is not a foe to wrestle with but a friend to embrace. Within the realm of Microsoft 365, such a world exists, and it's accessible through the Outlook calendar—a tool designed to simplify the intricate dance of scheduling.

The modern professional juggles numerous tasks, meetings, and deadlines. Without a robust system to manage these commitments, one risks the tumult of double-booked appointments or the embarrassment of forgotten engagements. A disorganized calendar is akin to a rudderless ship; both are prone to drift aimlessly, vulnerable to the caprices of the wind and waves.

What ensues from a cluttered schedule? Missed opportunities, strained relationships, and a tarnished reputation. Imagine the potential fallout from failing to appear at a crucial business meeting or forgetting a significant milestone in a client's journey. The cost of such oversights can be steep, not just in immediate losses but in long-term trust and credibility.

Enter the Outlook calendar, your digital timekeeper and personal assistant. It promises not just to avert the chaos of mismanaged time but to elevate your productivity to new heights. Through its intuitive interface, you can schedule meetings, set appointments, and create reminders that sync across all your devices, ensuring you're always attuned to the rhythm of your commitments.

To harness the full power of the Outlook calendar, one must first lay a foundation of understanding. Open Outlook, locate the Calendar button and click.

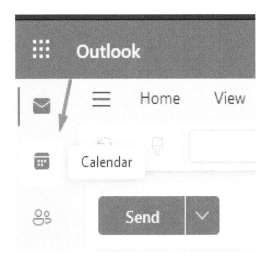

Begin with the basics: set your working hours, input public holidays, and mark personal time. This preliminary mapping of your time alerts others to when you're available and shields your personal hours from the encroachment of work. To do these, click the View tab and click 'Calendar settings'. Close the Settings window when you are done.

Now, let's delve into scheduling meetings. Click on the 'New event' button in the Home tab, a portal to collaborative timekeeping. You'll be greeted with fields begging for details. Who will attend? What is the agenda? When and where will it convene? As you populate these fields, consider the cadence of your invitees' days. Are they early risers, their minds sharpest with the dawn? Or do they thrive as the day wanes? Timing is a subtle art, and its mastery can enhance participation and engagement.

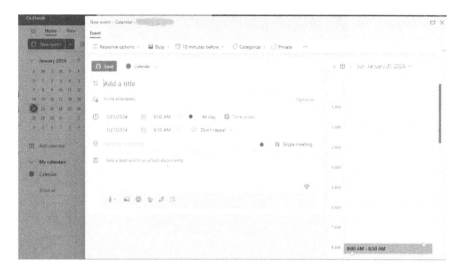

But what about those pesky reminders that seem to slip through the cracks of our memory? Do you recall that promise to follow up with a client in two weeks? With a few clicks, you can set a reminder that syncs across your phone, tablet, and computer. The Outlook calendar becomes your external memory, nudging you with notifications so that every commitment goes fulfilled.

As you venture forth in your journey with Microsoft 365, let the Outlook calendar be your guide. Embrace its potential to transform the way you manage time. With each event you schedule and each reminder you set, you're not just organizing your day—you're crafting a life where time is not an adversary but an ally, a precious resource to be wielded with precision and care.

Remember, the simple act of scheduling is but the first step in a grander ballet of time management. As you close this chapter, you are not merely a user of a digital tool—you are an architect of order, a conductor of time's symphony, ready to compose the days and weeks ahead with the deft touch of a maestro in the art of living.

CONTACTS: KEEPING TRACK OF CONNECTIONS

When the gears of daily life turn with the relentless ticks of a clock, staying connected within your network becomes a vital cog in professional and personal success. In the universe of Microsoft 365, Outlook stands as a beacon, illuminating the path to efficient contact management and task organization. This chapter delves into the art of using Outlook to foster connections and keep your to-dos in check, ensuring that no thread of communication frays or important task goes unnoticed.

Before embarking on this journey, ensure that you have:

- Internet access.

- Access to Outlook within Microsoft 365.

- Basic knowledge of Outlook's interface.

- A list of contacts and tasks you wish to manage.

The roadmap to achieving mastery over your contacts and tasks in Outlook includes several stops:

1. Navigating to the People section to manage contacts.

2. Adding and organizing contacts into meaningful categories.

3. Transitioning to the Tasks section to create and manage task lists.

4. Utilizing task categories and setting reminders to stay on track.

5. Syncing your contacts and tasks across devices for seamless access.

Let's unravel the intricacies of these steps with precision.

Firstly, navigate to the People section in Outlook. Here lies the heart of your connections, a hub where contact details reside.

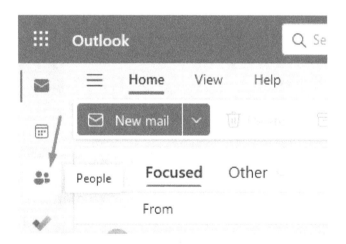

Once in People, adding a new contact is as simple as clicking 'New Contact' and filling in the blanks. Name, email, phone number, and more—each field is a thread binding you to your network.

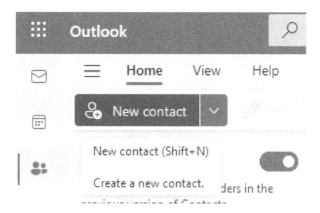

Now, imagine a tapestry of contacts, each with its unique hue. This is where categories come in. Assign colors to group contacts—colleagues in blue, clients in green, and personal connections in red. Suddenly, the tapestry gains clarity, and finding the right thread becomes effortless.

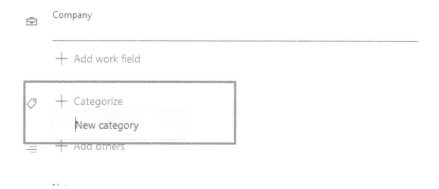

In conclusion, as the world spins on, let Outlook's contacts feature be the gravitational pull that keeps your network securely in orbit. With every new connection you save, you are not just managing information; you are building bridges and forging paths to a future of limitless potential.

CHAPTER 6 → ONEDRIVE: CONVENIENT WAY TO STORE, ACCESS AND SHARE FILES

NAVIGATING THE ONEDRIVE INTERFACE

Navigating to OneDrive and understanding its interface is essential for efficiently managing files and collaborating with others.

Once logged in, locate the App Launcher icon (usually represented by a grid or nine dots) in the upper left corner of the screen. Click on the App Launcher icon, and you should see a list of available Microsoft 365 applications. Find and click on the OneDrive icon. You will be redirected to the OneDrive interface, where you can manage your files and folders.

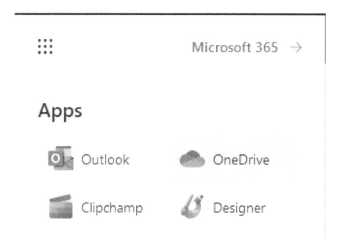

On the left side of the screen, you'll find the navigation pane. Here, you can access different sections of OneDrive, such as Files, Recent, Shared, and Recycle Bin. The navigation pane allows you to switch between different views and sections within OneDrive quickly.

The main area of the interface displays your files and folders. Files are organized in a grid or list view, depending on your preference. You can sort files by name, date modified, or file size and filter them by file type.

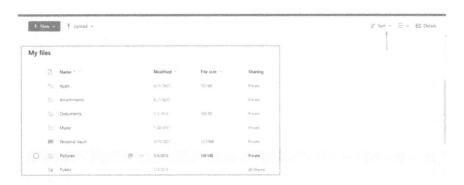

At the top of the interface, you'll find a toolbar with various options for managing files and folders. Options typically include buttons for uploading files, creating new folders, syncing files with your desktop, and sharing files with others.

Located at the top of the interface, the search bar allows you to quickly find specific files or folders by entering keywords or phrases. The search feature in OneDrive is powerful and can help you locate files even if you need help remembering their exact names.

When you hover over a file or folder, you'll see a set of action icons appear. These icons allow you to perform actions such as opening, downloading, sharing, moving, copying, or deleting files and folders.

Some versions of OneDrive may include a details pane on the right side of the interface. The details pane provides additional information about the selected file or folder, such as file size, sharing status, and activity history.

Above the file view, you'll find a breadcrumb trail that shows the current location within your OneDrive folder hierarchy. You can click on any part of the breadcrumb trail to navigate to a different folder.

My files > Pictures > **Screenshots**

Understanding the navigation and interface of OneDrive in Microsoft 365 allows users to efficiently manage files, collaborate with others, and access their content from anywhere with an internet connection.

UPLOADING AND ORGANIZING FILES

Uploading and organizing files in OneDrive is essential for maintaining a structured and efficient file storage system.

Uploading Files

Locate the folder where you want to upload your files. You can either choose an existing folder or create a new one by clicking on the "New" button and selecting "Folder".

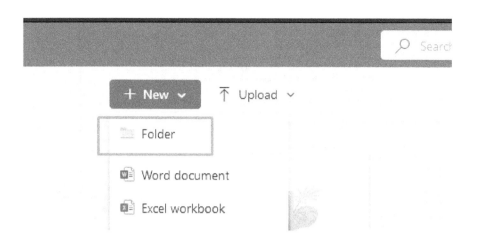

Drag the files from your computer's file explorer and drop them into the OneDrive interface in the web browser. Or click on the "Upload" button in the OneDrive interface and select "Files" or "Folder" to browse and choose the files you want to upload.

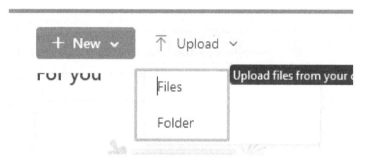

Depending on the size and number of files, the upload process may take some time. You can monitor the progress of uploads in the OneDrive interface. Once the upload is complete, you'll receive a confirmation message. Your files are now stored in OneDrive and accessible from any device with an internet connection.

Organizing Files

Organize your files by creating folders based on categories, projects, or any other relevant criteria. To create a new folder, click on the "New" button and select "Folder". Name the folder appropriately.

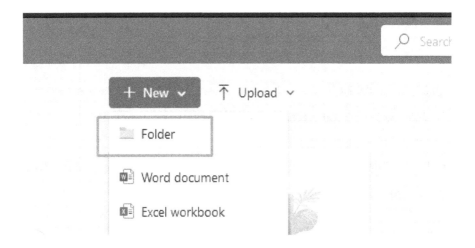

To organize existing files, select the files you want to move, click on the "Move to" button, and choose the destination folder. Alternatively, you can drag and drop files into the desired folder.

Right-click on a file or folder and select "Rename" to change its name. Choose descriptive names to identify files and folders easily.

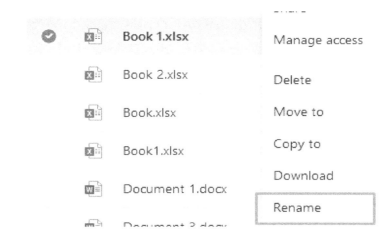

OneDrive allows you to sort files and folders by name, date modified, or file size. Use the sorting options to arrange files in a way that makes sense to you. You can also use the search bar to find specific files quickly.

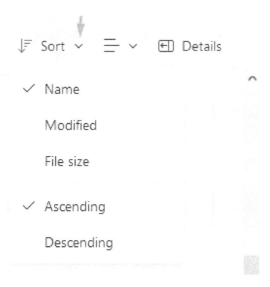

Add tags or metadata to files for better organization and searchability. You can add metadata properties to files to classify them based on specific attributes.

Regularly review and organize your files to keep your OneDrive workspace clutter-free and efficient. Delete or archive outdated files to free up space and improve productivity.

By following these steps, you can effectively upload and organize files in OneDrive, ensuring easy access, collaboration, and management of your digital assets.

SHARING AND COLLABORATION

Sharing and collaboration are key features of OneDrive that allow users to work together on files and projects seamlessly.

Sharing Files and Folders

Navigate to the file or folder you want to share within your OneDrive account. Select the file or folder, then click on the "Share" button in the toolbar at the top of the screen.

Enter the email addresses of the individuals you want to share the file or folder with. You can also enter a message to accompany the invitation. Choose whether recipients can view or edit the file. You can also set an expiration date for the link, after which it will no longer be accessible.

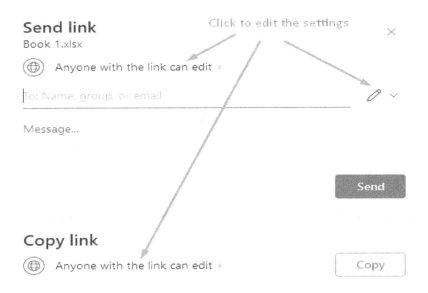

Click on the "Send" button to send the sharing invitation to the selected recipients.

Alternatively, you can copy the sharing link generated by OneDrive and share it via email, chat, or any other communication platform.

Collaborating in Real-Time

If you're collaborating on an Office document (Word, Excel, PowerPoint, etc.) stored in OneDrive, multiple users can edit the document simultaneously using Office Online or the desktop Office applications.

Changes made by one user are reflected in real-time for all collaborators. Each user's edits are highlighted with their respective color, allowing for easy identification.

Users can leave comments and feedback on documents, spreadsheets, and presentations to facilitate communication and collaboration.

OneDrive keeps track of version history for files, allowing users to view and restore previous versions if needed. This feature helps prevent accidental changes or loss of data.

OneDrive supports co-authoring, which enables multiple users to work on the same document simultaneously without interfering with each other's changes.

Managing Shared Content

Recipients can access shared files and folders by clicking on the link provided in the sharing invitation or email.

Users can view and edit permissions for shared files and folders, including adding or removing collaborators and changing access levels.

OneDrive provides activity logs and notifications to track changes and updates made to shared files and folders.

Owners of shared files and folders can revoke access or disable sharing links at any time. This helps maintain control over sensitive information and prevents unauthorized access.

Best Practices for Sharing and Collaboration

- Only share files and folders with trusted individuals or groups.
- Regularly review and manage sharing permissions to ensure security and privacy.
- Communicate effectively with collaborators to coordinate tasks and provide feedback.
- Use version history and backups to protect against data loss or accidental changes.

By leveraging the sharing and collaboration features of OneDrive, users can work together more efficiently, streamline workflows, and achieve better outcomes for their projects and initiatives.

CONCLUSION

As the final chapter of our digital journey comes to a close, one might pause and ponder, "What now?" After all, the expedition through the vast, intricate corridors of Microsoft 365 has been nothing short of remarkable, has it not?

Reflect on the beginning, where simple curiosity bloomed into a quest for mastery over the tools that compose this powerful suite. From the foundational bricks of Word's word processing to the complex data tapestries woven in Excel, every step taken was a stride toward efficiency and productivity. Did you not feel a surge of triumph when you pieced together your first PowerPoint presentation, each slide a testament to your growing skill?

Consider the paths traversed: Outlook's email labyrinth and OneDrive collaborative arenas. Each application is a realm with its own rules and its magic. The beauty of Microsoft 365 is not just in the individual prowess of each application but also in the symphony they create when working in concert.

As you move forward, remember that Microsoft 365 is not a static entity; it evolves, as do you. New features will emerge, old ones will be polished, and your knowledge will need to adapt. The learning thus never truly ends. It's an ongoing process, a perpetual cycle of discovery and mastery.

Take a moment now to envision the future. How will the skills you've honed shape your path? What new projects await, eager for the touch of your expertise? There is a world of possibility at your fingertips, a canvas of digital potential.

In the silence that follows, know that this conclusion is but a comma in the narrative of your learning. The story continues, and you, the protagonist, are equipped with the knowledge, the skills, and the confidence to write the ensuing chapters.

So, dear reader, as you turn the page on this guide, remember: the true power of Microsoft 365 lies not within the software itself but within the person who wields it. You are the architect of your digital destiny, the sculptor of your virtual vision. Go forth and create, for the world awaits the imprint of your unique brilliance.

Thank you for your purchase! If you enjoyed this book, check out these other titles. Happy reading!